GLORIA ESTEFAN

gloria!

Project Manager: Jeannette DeLisa
Art Layout: Joseph Klucar
Album Art: © 1998 Sony Music Entertainment Inc.
Photography: Adolfo Perez Butrón
Back Cover Photo: Matthew Rolston

WARNER BROS. PUBLICATIONS - THE GLOBAL LEADER IN PRINT
USA: 15800 NW 48th Avenue, Miami, FL 33014

WARNER/CHAPPELL MUSIC

NUOVA CARISCH

INTERNATIONAL MUSIC PUBLICATIONS LIMITED

CANADA: 40 SHEPPARD AVE. WEST, SUITE 800
TORONTO, ONTARIO, M2N 6K9
SCANDINAVIA: P.O. BOX 533, VENDEVAGEN 85 B
S-182 15, DANDERYD, SWEDEN
AUSTRALIA: P.O. BOX 353
3 TALAVERA ROAD, NORTH RYDE N.S.W. 2113

ITALY: VIA CAMPANIA, 12
20098 S. GIULIANO MILANESE (MI)
ZONA INDUSTRIALE SESTO ULTERIANO
SPAIN: MAGALLANES, 25
28015 MADRID
FRANCE: 25 RUE DE HAUTEVILLE, 75010 PARIS

ENGLAND: SOUTHEND ROAD,
WOODFORD GREEN, ESSEX IG8 8HN
GERMANY: MARSTALLSTR. 8, D-80539 MUNCHEN
DENMARK: DANMUSIK, VOGNMAGERGADE 7
DK 1120 KOBENHAVNK

OYE

Words and Music by
GLORIA ESTEFAN, EMILIO ESTEFAN, JR.,
RANDALL BARLOW and ANGIE CHIRINO

12

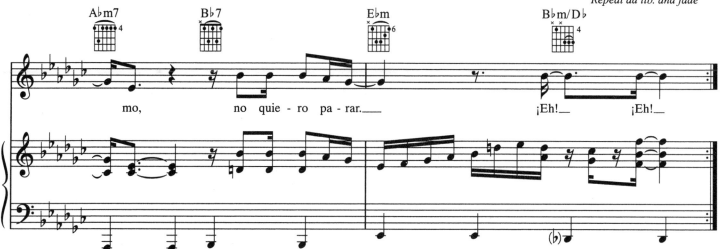

mo,   no quie - ro pa - rar.___   ¡Eh!___   ¡Eh!___

Spanish Lyrics:
Mi cuerpo pide, oye (My body wants)

Oye, mi cuerpo pide salsa (Hey, my body wants salsa)
Y con este ritmo (And with this rhythm)
Vamos a bailar (Let's dance)

Oye, mi cuerpo pide salsa (Hey, my body wants salsa)
Y con este ritmo (And with this rhythm)
No quiero parar (I don't wanna stop)

Oye
Que estás haciendo
Estoy cayendo
La fuerza se me vá

Dime
Que estás pensando
Te estoy mirando
Me gustas más y más, cariño

Con cada latido de mi corazón
Me enamoro mucho más de tí
Amorcito, acércate un poquito más
Ya verás como te vas a enamorar de mí

Oye, mi cuerpo pide salsa
Y con este ritmo
Vamos a bailar

Oye, mi cuerpo pide salsa
Y con este ritmo
No quiero parar

Dale
No tengas miedo,
Mi cuerpo entero
Te quiero entregar

Rico
Bien pegadito
Tan suavecito
Te voy a conquistar, cariño

Son tus ojos que me hacen enloquecer
Con un beso pierdo la razón
Siento esta locura y ya no sé que hacer
Es que tu cariño hace vibrar mi corazón

Oye, mi cuerpo pide salsa
Y con este ritmo
Vamos a bailar

Oye, mi cuerpo pide salsa
Y con este ritmo
No quiero parar

HEAVEN'S WHAT I FEEL

Words and Music by
KIKE SANTANDER

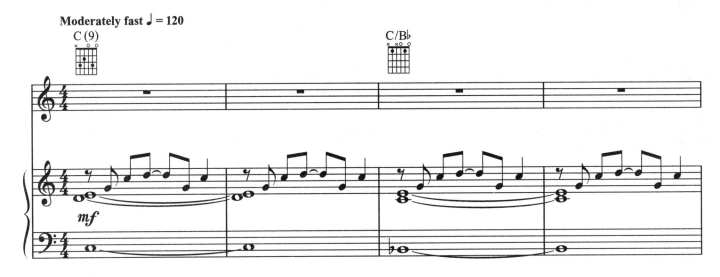

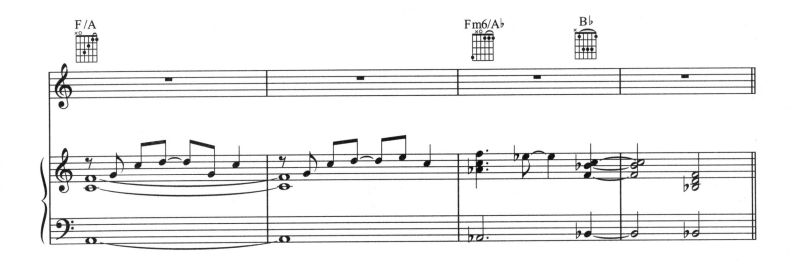

%. *Chorus:*

I was not___ sup - posed_____ to fall in love with you.___

__ I have some - one_ else,_ and some - one else_ is lov -

ing you._ And I was not___ sup - posed_____ to let this

love get through.___ So let me say_ for real,_____

To Coda

REAL WOMAN

Words and Music by
GLORIA ESTEFAN, EMILIO ESTEFAN, JR.,
and LAWRENCE P. DERMER

What you need is a real, real___ wom-an to-night.

A real___ wom-an to-night;___ some-one that does___ you right,___

Real Woman - 6 - 2
0278B

a real___ wom-an to-night.___ (Real wom-an, a real, real wom-an.)

N.C.

To Coda

Verse:
1. You don't know what's good for you,___ and all the girls you had
2. What a shame you wast-ed time;___ make it up and tell me

Repeat ad lib. and fade

DON'T LET THIS MOMENT END

Words and Music by
GLORIA ESTEFAN, EMILIO ESTEFAN, JR.,
LAWRENCE P. DERMER and ROBERT D. BLADES

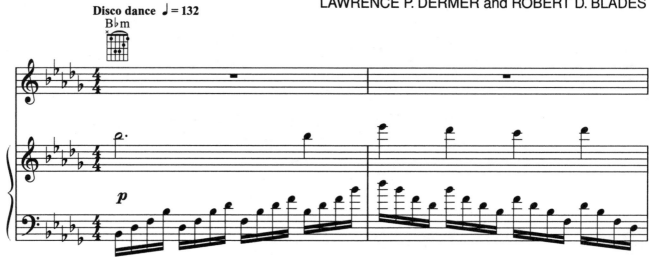

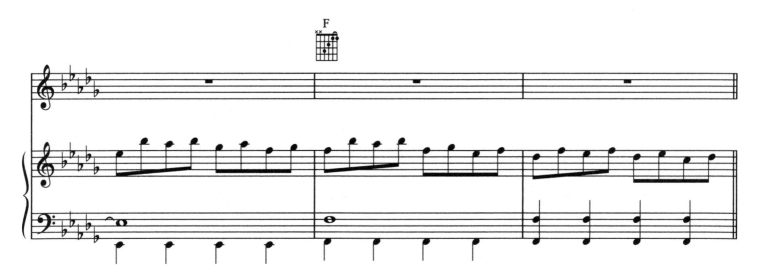

Don't Let This Moment End - 12 - 1
0278B

Bridge:

Can we make this mo - ment last for - ev - er? (For - ev - er.) Tell me if you feel the way I do. Oh! (Don't let this

Don't Let This Moment End - 12 - 10
0278B

I JUST WANNA BE HAPPY

Words and Music by
LAWRENCE P. DERMER

Chorus:

46

FEELIN'

Words and Music by
LAWRENCE P. DERMER

Verse:

1. And when you give what's in your heart to_____ the
2. When ev - 'ry look and eve - ry touch makes_____ you

one you_ love,_____ you want them_ to give_____
come un - done,_____ and you can't_ be - lieve_____

their love back_ to you._____
this feel - in'_____ is real,_____

When eve - ry kiss and ev - 'ry smile mean___ the world to__ you,___
and when the sound of some-one's name gives___ you but - ter - flies,___

CUBA LIBRE

Words by
GLORIA ESTEFAN and EMILIO ESTEFAN, JR.

Music by
GLORIA ESTEFAN, EMILIO ESTEFAN, JR.
and KIKE SANTANDER

Bright latin beat ♩ = 120

The place that I come from___ I bare - ly re-mem-ber.___ The place that I come from___ I bare - ly re-mem-ber.___ But the soul of my peo-ple___ will be with me for-ev-er.___ The

Cuba Libre - 8 - 1
0278B

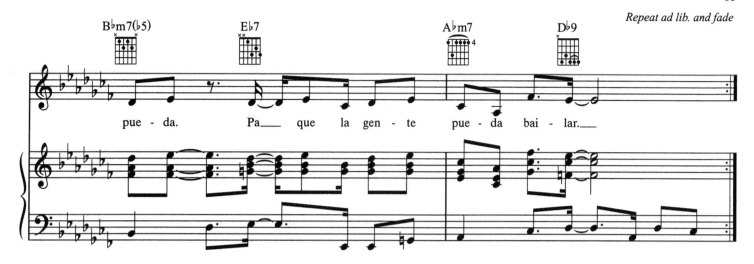

Repeat ad lib. and fade

pue - da. Pa___ que la gen - te pue - da bai - lar.___

Spanish Lyrics:
Curioso destino
Que aún me separa
De mi tierra adorada
Que no veo desde niña

No puedo olvidar
Eres parte de mí
Te quiero ver feliz

Un mar de recuerdos
Azota mi mente
De pueblos y gentes
Que yo he conocido

Curioso destino
Que aún me separa
Curioso destino
Que aún me separa
De mi tierra adorada
Que no veo desde niña
De mi tierra adorada
Que no veo desde niña

No puedo olvidar
Eres parte de mí
Te quiero ver feliz

Quiero mi Cuba libre
Pa' que la gente pueda
Pa' que mi gente pueda bailar

A veces no entiendo
Lo mucho que extraño
Que a pesar de los años
Te sigo queriendo
Sigo esperando
Yo te sigo soñando
Comparto tus penas
Estoy contigo llorando

No puedo olvidar
Eres parte de mí
Te quiero ver feliz

Quiero mi Cuba libre
Pa' que la gente pueda
Pa' que mi gente pueda bailar

CORAZON PROHIBIDO

Words by
GLORIA ESTEFAN and KIKE SANTANDER

Music by
KIKE SANTANDER

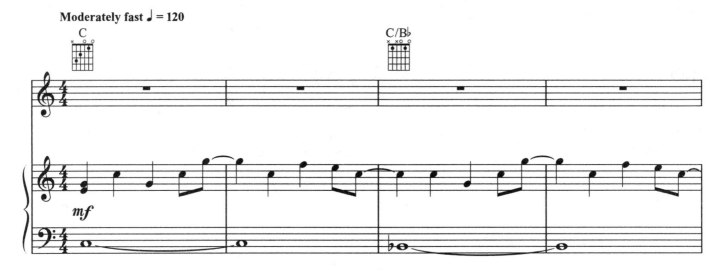

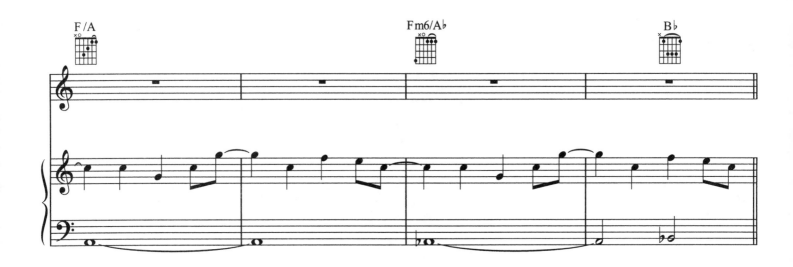

1. Un a - mor___ que se_a - due - ñó de mí,___

2. *See additional lyrics*

Corazon Prohibido - 7 - 2
0278B

68

Corazon Prohibido - 7 - 3
0278B

%. *Chorus:*

Nun - ca_i - ma - gi - né_____ po - der a - mar - te_a - sí._____

Tie - nes o - tro_a - mor,_____ Y_o - tro_a - mor__ me tie -

ne_a mí.__ Y nun - ca yo___ so - ñé_____ que - rer - te

tan - to_a - sí._____ Que cul - pa ten - go yo_____ si

To Coda ⊕

de - scu - bri el___ a - mor___ só - lo___ por

ti.___

Verse 2:
Como hacer al corazón saber
Cuando llega el sentimiento,
Si el amor es un camino incierto.
Este amor que siento en mí nacer,
Me devuelve aquel secreto,
Que una vez temí perder.
Por ti yo he roto
Las reglas del amor,
Jamás pensé perder el corazón.
Y me atrapa esta locura,
Que me enciende, que me nubla,
Nada puedo hacer para es capar de ti.
(Coro)

DON'T RELEASE ME

Words and Music by
LAWRENCE P. DERMER
Rap by
WYCLEF JEAN

Show me how to find the way__ to par - a - dise,__

Rap lyrics:
A-one-two, a-one-two.
(Yeah, yeah, yi-yi-yeah, yeah.)
I'd like to introduce to you
(Back by popular demand)

Wyclef Jean with Gloria Estefan.
When the Cubans meet the Hatians and Sicilians,
Hold your corner, hold your corner.
For all the thugs who've ever been in love.

Hey, yo, this one goes out for the Cuban Kings and Queens.
You ever fell in love with a pretty serpentine?
I met her at the club, yes, down with my pager.
Ask her what's her name, she said, "Gloria."

Where you from? "Cuba." What you do? "I'm a singer."
I pulled out my stash; she said, "Are you a dealer from Havana?"
No, no. Yo, can I buy you a tequila?
She said, "Hell no, I'll take a piña colada."

Now, with one drink, I'll put her in a spell.
I'm huntin' the kid like a cheetah hunts a gazelle.
I know it's wrong, but I'm waitin' for her mistake
So I can take over like the devil's advocate.
(To Chorus:)

DON'T STOP

Words and Music by
EMILIO ESTEFAN, JR., TONY MORAN,
and ANGIE CHIRINO

Don't Stop - 9 - 1
0278B

Ooh.

Bridge:

Can't think a - bout____ to - mor - row's_ fears,____ 'cause to -

DON'T RELEASE ME
(Wyclef Jean Remix)

Words and Music by
LAWRENCE P. DERMER
Rap by
WYCLEF JEAN

Moderate rap ♩ = 96

Rap intro:

N.C.

Rap: See additional lyrics

Oh.____

1.2.   ‖ 3.

Verse:

B♭m7   E♭m7   B♭m7

1. Please,   don't re - lease__ me,   don't re - lease__ me   from this

2. *See additional lyrics*

94

Rap 2nd time:
Gloria is in the place, and-uh, and-uh,

go?

(Inst. solo . . .

the East Coast is in the place, and-uh, and-uh, the West Coast is in the place, and-uh, and-uh.

I wan - na let

. . . end solo)

Chorus:

go. *(First time only)*   But I can't let   go.   Do you wan - na let

Repeat ad lib. and fade

Rap intro:
Back by popular demand,
At the Copacabana,
Gloria Estefan,
On the new drum,
With The Refugees.
Get off the wall, feel this one.
You ready?

This one goes out for the Cuban Kings and Queens,
Thugs fallin' in love with Latin serpentines.
I met her at the club, guess down with a pager.
I ask her what's her name, she said, "Gloria."

Where you from? "Cuba." What you do? "I'm a singer."
She looked at me and said, "Do you wanna let go?"
No, no, but can I get you a tequila?
She said, "Hell no, I'll take a piña colada." Uh-huh.

With one sip, I got her in a spell.
I'm huntin' her, kin, like a cheetah hunts a gazelle.
I know it's wrong, but I'm waitin' for her to break
So I can take over like the devil's advocate.

Verse 2:
Please,
Don't release me,
Don't release me
From this spell you've got me under.
I said
Please,
Don't release me,
No, don't release me
From this spell you've got me under.
I wanna find the way to paradise,
And you can take me there.
You know I feel like I could rise above the crowd,
And I don't wanna come down.
(To Chorus:)

LUCKY GIRL

Words and Music by
EMILIO ESTEFAN, JR. and LAWRENCE P. DERMER

Latin dance beat ♩= 126

There are some girls who'd nev - er___ take___ a chance,

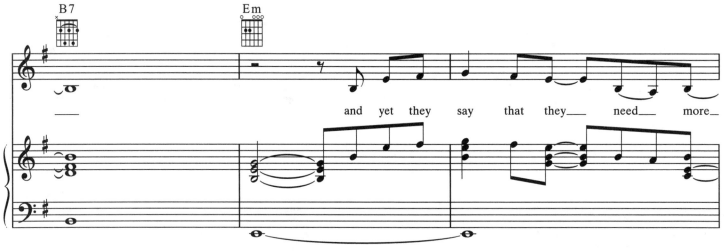

and yet they say that they___ need___ more

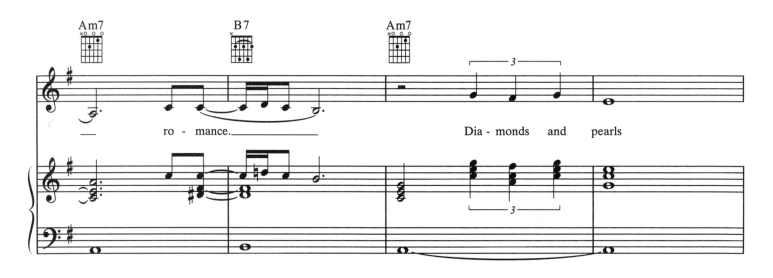

ro - mance.___ Dia - monds and pearls

Lucky Girl - 9 - 1
0278B

102

(You do it to me like it's nev-er been done be-fore..

D.S. %al Coda

You do it to me like it's nev-er been done be-fore._____

Coda Am7

_____ (Such a luck-y.)

B7

I'm gon-na give it, give it, give it all to you._

Em

(Such a luck-y girl._____)

Am7

Oh,

Lucky Girl - 9 - 8
0278B

TOUCHED BY AN ANGEL

Words by
GLORIA ESTEFAN and EMILIO ESTEFAN, JR.

Music by
GLORIA ESTEFAN, EMILIO ESTEFAN, JR.
and KIKE SANTANDER

d By an Angel - 7 - 1